AMERICA'S TEST KITCHEN

Mitsy
the Oven Mitt
Goes to School

A Story About Being ~~Nervous~~ Brave!

By Chad Chenail

Illustrated by Gabi Homonoff

Hi!
I'm Mitsy!

And I'm an oven mitt.
Obviously.

I'm not JUST
an oven mitt, though!

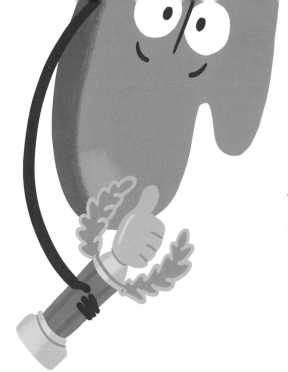

I'm ALSO a champion thumb wrestler. I'm an excellent listener.

I love playing hot potato, learning secret handshakes, and doing the wave.

Also . . . I'm a bit of a worrier.

I don't tell everyone this. But I'd like to think we're friends . . . even though I am an oven mitt, and you are a person reading a book. You see, I get . . . **NERVOUS.**

Especially around ovens. Yes, I am an oven mitt, but I do *not* like ovens.

I live in Mitt City. Technically it's a glove and mitten factory. But it's where so many hand coverings like me call home.

I've lived here my entire life. But soon . . . I'm leaving. You won't be surprised to hear that I'm PRETTY **NERVOUS.**

It all started with a letter that came in the mail . . .

I thought it was the national thread count, or maybe that I'd won that fabric softener giveaway I'd entered! Until I saw the return address.

Mitsy
221 Baker Street
Mitt City

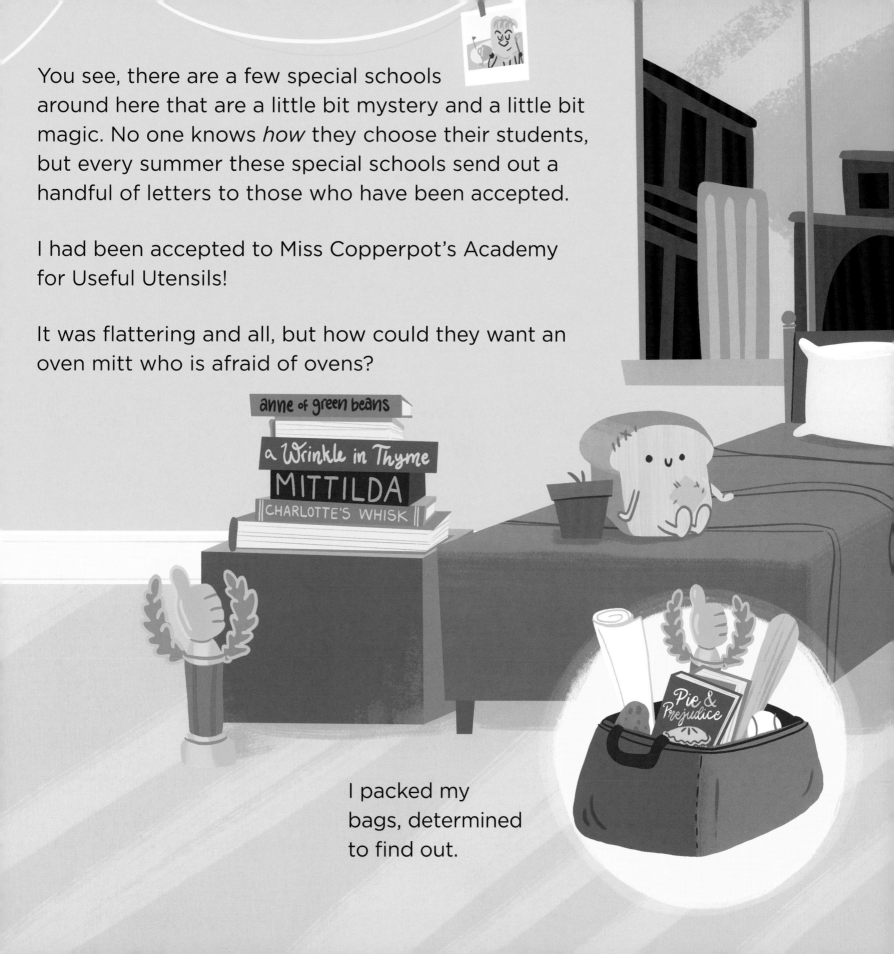

You see, there are a few special schools around here that are a little bit mystery and a little bit magic. No one knows *how* they choose their students, but every summer these special schools send out a handful of letters to those who have been accepted.

I had been accepted to Miss Copperpot's Academy for Useful Utensils!

It was flattering and all, but how could they want an oven mitt who is afraid of ovens?

anne of green beans

a Wrinkle in Thyme

MITTILDA

CHARLOTTE'S WHISK

Pie & Prejudice

I packed my bags, determined to find out.

And so . . . here we are. As my bus pulls into Miss Copperpot's Academy for Useful Utensils, I am feeling . . . **NERVOUS.**

I see kitchen utensils everywhere! Forks and sporks, big pots and small pans. But I don't see a single oven mitt.

A spoon leads me
to my room.

It's big. And empty.

At least it's quiet here—so quiet that I can hear my heart beating in my finely quilted chest. Can you hear it, too?

Thump, thump, thump.

Golly, my first class starts soon. I need to know what I'm getting myself into!

WHAT IF THERE ARE OVENS?!

Wait. I know that I'm just an oven mitt telling a story in a book and you're just the person reading this book, but maybe you can help. Can you do me a favor and check out my first class? It's on the next page.

Just turn the page, give it a quick peek, and let me know if there are any ovens in today's lesson. Pretty please?

You mean to tell me it's a room FULL of ovens?!

IT'S CALLED OVENS 101?

Golly. It's OK. Just breathe, Mitsy. Happy safety thoughts in! Tragic oven thoughts out. Gah. I guess there's nothing left to do but go?

Here goes nothing.

"Welcome to Ovens 101. For your first lesson, please split off into groups of two. And find an oven!"

That's my teacher, Ms. Holder. She seems nice enough.

Maybe nobody will pick me! Or maybe there won't be enough ovens, and I'll have to sit this one out!

"Do you have a partner yet?"
I hear a quiet voice say.
"I'm Pat. Pat Shula."

"Do you know how to thumb
wrestle?" I hear myself ask.

What kind
of a question
is that?
Welp. My
life is over.

This is it for me.
It was nice reading
with you, friend.

Hope you enjoyed
the book. Goodbye
and good luck.

"Maybe you can show me
how!" says Pat, which
makes me smile.

Ms. Holder snaps her fingers, and all the ovens in the room turn on at once.

I snap mine, too, to see if I can turn them back off, but I guess that's not how it works.

I feel more **NERVOUS.**

"Before we begin, let me remind you that an oven is not a toy," says Ms. Holder. "Today, we are just going to feel the heat. TOMORROW, we will carefully remove a cookie from inside the oven."

That night, I toss and turn for hours, like I'm in the spin cycle at the laundromat.

After what feels like forever, I decide to get up. A little walk will help, right?

I turn this way and that, past paintings of countless heroes who were probably never nervous a day in their lives.

I look up and realize
I am very, very lost.

I sit on the floor and start to cry.

Mitsy dear, are you all right?

I look up to see Ms. Holder's very kind smile.

"No, I'm not," I sniffle back. "I might be an oven mitt, but . . . I'm afraid of ovens! I'm like an airplane who's afraid of heights! Or a life jacket who can't swim."

"Can I tell you a secret?" Ms. Holder asks. "Being nervous makes it possible for us to be brave."

"Brave?"

"Brave. If we never felt nervous, then we could never be brave!

"Next time you are feeling nervous, think about that feeling as an opportunity to do something brave. Learn how to do that, and you can accomplish anything.

Now, it's very late, and you need to go off to bed. We have a big day tomorrow—chop-chop!"

The next day arrives faster than a round of rock paper scissors, and I am back at my oven with Pat.

"Inside each oven I've placed a cookie," says Ms. Holder. "I'd like you to safely take the cookie out of the oven."

Here comes that **NERVOUSNESS** again.

I glance at Ms. Holder. Being **NERVOUS** is an opportunity to be brave. Golly. I can see the cookie in there. Think I can do this? I guess there's only one way to find out.

Let me take a deep breath first, though. Happy safety thoughts in. Tragic oven thoughts out. GAH! OK!

I'm **brave!**

Chewy Chocolate Chip Cookies

MAKES 12 cookies

TIME 50 minutes, plus cooling time

Prepare Ingredients

1 cup (5 ounces) plus 2 tablespoons all-purpose flour

¼ teaspoon baking soda

¼ teaspoon salt

½ cup packed (3½ ounces) light brown sugar

6 tablespoons unsalted butter, melted and cooled

¼ cup (1¾ ounces) sugar

1 large egg

1 teaspoon vanilla extract

¾ cup (4½ ounces) bittersweet or semisweet chocolate chips

Gather Baking Equipment

Rimmed baking sheet

Parchment paper

2 bowls (1 large, 1 medium)

Whisk

Rubber spatula

1-tablespoon measuring spoon

Oven mitts

Cooling rack

Spatula

Start Baking!

1 Adjust oven rack to lower-middle position and heat oven to 325 degrees. Line rimmed baking sheet with parchment paper.

2 In medium bowl, whisk together flour, baking soda, and salt.

3 In large bowl, whisk brown sugar, melted butter, and sugar until smooth. Add egg and vanilla and whisk until well combined.

4 Add flour mixture and use rubber spatula to stir until just combined and no streaks of flour are visible. Add chocolate chips and stir until evenly combined. (If dough is very sticky, refrigerate for 15 to 30 minutes before proceeding with step 5.)

5 Use your hands to roll dough into 12 balls (about 2 tablespoons each). Place dough balls on parchment-lined baking sheet, leaving about 2 inches between dough balls and arranging them in staggered rows so they don't melt into each other.

6 Place baking sheet in oven. Bake cookies until edges are set and beginning to brown but centers are still soft and puffy, 15 to 20 minutes.

7 Use oven mitts to remove baking sheet from oven and place on cooling rack (ask an adult for help). Let cookies cool on baking sheet for 10 minutes.

8 Use spatula to transfer cookies directly to cooling rack and let cool for 5 minutes before serving.

Library of Congress Cataloging-in-Publication Data has been applied for

ISBN 978-1-948703-76-5

AMERICA'S TEST KITCHEN
21 Drydock Avenue, Suite 210E, Boston, MA 02210

Printed in Canada
10 9 8 7 6 5 4 3 2 1

Distributed by Penguin Random House
Publisher Services

Hey grown-ups, do you and your young chefs want to bake these Chewy Chocolate Chip Cookies with me? Check out our bonus audio cook-along! Here's how to listen:

1. Open your cell phone camera, and point it at this QR code.

2. Click the link that appears at the top of your screen, or go to **www.atkkids.com/MitsyGoesToSchool** if that's not working.

3. Gather your ingredients, press play, and enjoy!